MAUI

A Picture Book to Remember Her by

CRESCENT BOOKS
NEW YORK

CLB1786
©1987 Colour Library Books Ltd., Guildford, Surrey, England.
Printed and bound in Barcelona, Spain by Cronion, S.A.
1987 edition published by Crescent Books, distributed by Crown Publishers, Inc.
ISBN 0 517 62920 8
h g f e d c b a

Southeast of Honolulu lies the tropical island of Maui. Second largest in the Hawaiian group, Maui was once two separate volcanic islands. Today, an isthmus, built up of material eroded from the two islands, connects the West Maui Mountains to Haleakala, giving Maui its nickname of the Valley Island. Steeped in myth, Maui was named after the legendary god who dragged the Hawaiian Islands up out of the sea, brought fire to their shores, and took the sun prisoner in order to lengthen the islanders' hours of fishing.

The island offers a wide variety of landscapes. Most visitors imagine a Pacific island paradise, and they will not be disappointed. Along the shores can be glimpsed white, sandy beaches, wild surf and palm trees, while coastal roads are marked by sumptuous cliffs, cascading waterfalls and the greens of lush tropical forests. Fields of sugarcane cover Maui's central plains, and cane and pineapple plantations clothe its foothills. When Captain Cook arrived in 1778, sugarcane was already growing wild, having been brought by canoe to Hawaii by the first Polynesians to settle here, around AD 400.

Eastern Maui presents another face, its scenery dominated by the dormant volcano, Haleakala, which rises majestically to over 10,000 feet. Haleakala's ruggedly beautiful crater suggests a moonscape, at its most spectacular at sunset or sunrise, when the movement of sun and clouds over its surfaces creates an eerie world of constantly changing color. Lichen, sandalwood, fern and the silversword plant grow within the crater's twenty-one-mile circumference, and the nene, a small Hawaiian goose, is glimpsed occasionally in the crater's well-watered areas. The cool, fertile lower slopes of the volcano are grazed by livestock, or planted with vegetables and flowers to supply the islands' markets. Elsewhere on its slopes the landscape changes again – to scented, silvery eucalyptus groves which fuse with the haze of purple-flowered jacaranda trees.

The island of Maui has a colorful history. Lahaina, for instance, on the west coast of the island, has been settled and visited by kings, missionaries and whalers, whose contrasting legacies are still felt in this old plantation town. Kamehameha the Great built a residence here, after having beaten Maui's chiefs in battle in 1790. In the 1820s some of the first missionaries from Boston landed at Lahaina and by the middle of the century they had irrevocably changed Hawaiian culture, building houses, churches, schools and trading posts, and even introducing a written language. Also in the mid-century, whalers from America came in droves to winter in this little port, and in turn impressed their stamp upon the island.

Although the western coast of Maui has experienced a big building boom in recent years and is now largely geared to tourism, the north eastern shore of the island offers many reminders of the old, colorful Hawaii. Little villages like Keanae and Wailua are found down small side-roads off the main coastal route, and here the easy pace and quiet charm of early island life still continues, the villagers responding with warmth and hospitality to visitors. Old Hawaii can be savored even in the commercial and business hub of the island, which centers around Maui's two major towns, Wailuku and Kahului, both situated on the northern end of the isthmus. The town of Wailuki lies on the tranquil slopes of the West Maui Mountains, at the mouth of the scenic Iao Valley, and is the older of the two adjoining towns. Its narrow, hilly streets, wooden shops and restful, tree-clad residential roads, recall old Hawaii, while its new developments blend attractively with its old quarters. The picturesque town of Kahului, Maui's deep sea port, lies on the coast alongside Kahului Bay. Here the onlooker can watch freighters being loaded with cargoes of sugar, pineapple, or molasses, as they have been since Maui's plantation economy developed in the first half of this century.

Today Maui is a holiday haven and draws tourists from all over the world in search of beautiful scenery, a warm climate and balmy sea breezes. The island's luxury resorts, golf courses and cosmopolitan shopping offer every modern amenity that the visitor could wish for. However, Maui has so much more: its scenery changes so completely as the visitor rounds the next corner, that he feels he has entered a magical landscape, surrounded by evidence of a history which encompasses New England Protestantism, heady whaling days and the richness of the Polynesian culture.

Facing page: the beach beside Whaler's Village in Kaanapali, on Maui's west coast.

Facing page: red anthuriums, (top) plumeria blooms, (above) a Chilean jasminum flower and (right) a dwarf poinciana. Overleaf: (main picture) Kahana Beach, and (inset right) Honolua Bay. Surfers (inset left) are attracted to Maui's beaches from all over the world.

Kaanapali (previous pages and facing page), on the west coast, has a beach three miles long. This part of the island is famous for its colorful sunsets, which are as spectacular as they are regular. Kaanapali also offers two fine golf courses, swimming pools, a tennis club, restaurants and nightly entertainment. There is also a railway station from which runs the open-sided, 1890-style steam train of the Lahaina-Kaanapali & Pacific Railway. The narrow gauge tracks run for 6 miles through sugar cane plantations, past the south golf course and across a 400-foot-long trestle. The west coast of Maui offers excellent surf (right). Below: the third smallest of the islands, Lanai, as seen from Wahikuli Beach Park. More than 12,000 acres of the land on this extinct volcano are cultivated for fruit production. Overleaf: sunbathing near Whaler's Village, Kaanapali.

Left and below: the beach by Whaler's Village, Kaanapali, with Lanai in the background. The Whaler's Village Museum and shopping centre (facing page) is set in 8 acres of land in south Kaanapali. This architecturally-fascinating complex has much to offer visitors throughout the year, including many and varied restaurants, a cinema, a beautiful Hawaiian landscaped garden and an amphitheater. The museum features a forty-foot-long sperm whale skeleton amongst other exhibits celebrating Maui's long association with the great mammal. Whale watching may still be enjoyed in the winter months as the humpbacks migrate to their Hawaiian breeding grounds. The center's shops offer a colorful range of local goods, including ancient and modern pieces of scrimshaw work (engravings in ivory, bone and whales' teeth), clothing and other handcrafted Hawaiian gifts. Overleaf: sailing-craft silhouetted against the sunset off Wahikuli Beach Park.

Previous pages: Wahikuli Beach Park.
Top: sugar cane fields beside the
Honoapiilani Highway, and (facing page
top) Victorian-style Lahaina Station, part
of the old sugar cane haulage line. Facing
page bottom: a bird of paradise flower in
one of Maui's gardens (above and right).

Previous pages: the West Maui Mountains provide a dramatic backdrop for some of the island's sugar cane plantations. Pineapples (inset) provide Maui's other major crop. These pages: historic Lahaina, the former whaling capital of the Pacific and the place where Kamehameha the Great built a residence after conquering Maui in 1790. The town's restoration plan has encouraged the refurbishment and recreation of structures from its 19th- and early-20th-century history including the balconied Pioneer Inn (above), which dates from 1901. In the 1850s the port provided winter shelter for thousands of whalers. Nowadays the harbor is occupied by pleasure craft (left). The Lin Wa glass bottom boat (facing page top) explores the local coral reefs daily. Behind it stands the Courthouse, which now houses the Lahaina Art Gallery and was built in 1859 with stone from Hale Piula (the old court house, destroyed by a gale in 1858). Facing page bottom: a hotel on the shore.

Previous pages: Lahaina Harbor against the cloud-topped West Maui Mountains. The dark foliage behind the Courthouse (center) is that of the largest banyan tree on the island. Right: a giant bronze Buddha, the focal point of the Japanese Cultural Park of the Lahaina Jodo Mission just north of the town, erected to commemorate the centenary of the arrival of the first Japanese plantation laborers in 1868. Below: a spectacular catch is admired in Lahaina harbor. The turn-of-the-century Pioneer Inn (facing page top), in Lahaina, was west Maui's only visitor accommodation until the late 1950s. It has been restored and enlarged in keeping with Lahaina's conservation program (a joint effort of state and local government with the Lahaina Restoration Foundation) and is full of whaling artifacts. The Carthaginian II (facing page bottom), also part of this program, is a replica of a typical whaling ship and acts as a floating museum, containing the "World of the Whale" exhibit.

Previous pages and left: the Heritage Gardens in Kepaniwai Park. The name Kepaniwai, meaning "damming of the waters", originates from the myth which tells of how the Iao stream was choked here with the bodies of soldiers slain when Kamehameha conquered Maui in 1790. These days it is a place of peaceful beauty containing tributes in landscape to the cultures instrumental in Hawaii's growth. In the nearby Iao Valley State Park, well-marked footpaths lead through lush, aromatic vegetation. Though usually shrouded in cool mountain mist, the surrounding peaks may afford views as far as Kahului Bay. The valley is dominated by the Iao Needle (facing page and below left), a great lava monolith rising resplendent in green, flanked by the walls of the Puu Kukui Crater. Legend has it that this spectacle was created by the fire goddess, Pele. Below: a roadside shrine and (overleaf) a pagoda in the Japanese Heritage Garden, Kepaniwai Park.

The lava shore of the Keanae Peninsula (previous pages left), on the northwest coast of the island, is constantly washed by Pacific surf. Previous pages right and overleaf: fields of taro form a patchwork on the land at Keanae. Thirty-two varieties of this rootcrop may be found at the nearby arboretum, along with many other plants both native and foreign to Hawaii. These pages: aerial views of the unspoilt north coastline.

Hawaii's climate supports many beautiful tropical flowers. Facing page: (top) an unusual ixora and (bottom) pentas. Top: the glory bush, (top right) plumeria, (right) the rocket protea and (above) an hibiscus, Hawaii's national flower. Overleaf: two more fine plumerias, the blooms of which are used to make garlands.

The Hana Highway runs for over 50 miles along the north coast, offering some of the most spectacular and varied views on Maui, the 'Island of Many Contrasts'. Jagged black rocks and spitting surf give way to narrow valleys and freshwater falls as the road winds towards Hana. Keanae (above) and the Haipuaena Falls (facing page) are passed en route. Overleaf: a view at sunset from Kahului Bay, looking across to Kahakuloa Head.

Right: flame of the forest. Waianapanapa State Park
(remaining pictures and overleaf) is known for its
tropical vegetation and dramatic black beach, and
legend tells of the murder of a princess in one of its
sea-caves. Above and overleaf: Queen Emma lilies.

'Ohe'o Gulch or Seven Pools (these pages), just inside Haleakala National Park, is a superb site for picnics and swimming. From the bridge, pools may be seen in both directions, toppling seawards. Overleaf: the West Maui Mountains seen from Highway 377.

Haleakala, the volcano that formed the east of the island, has been dormant since 1790. The crater (facing page), a great depression on the volcano's southwest flank, harbors many unusual sights, including that of the exquisite silversword plant (this page).

Previous pages: Haleakala National Park. (Left top) looking west across the park at sunset and (left bottom) the cindery crater. (Right top) the Hana Highway, winding along the coast of northern Maui, and (right bottom) flowers growing where molten lava flowed in Haleakala's active days. Haleakala National Park (left and facing page) offers three rustic cabins and a visitors' center in the crater for the use of explorers who wish to prolong their stay in its remarkable landscape. Hiking is popular here, despite the tremendous altitude. Science City (below), a spectacle in itself, affords magnificent panoramic views. Facing page: (top) a view from the summit of Haleakala across the highway and the crater. The drive to the top passes through cane fields and pineapple spreads, pasture and quite possibly layers of cloud as it twists and turns ever upwards. (Bottom) the outlines of Hawaii Island beyond the crater's old lava flows. Overleaf: Waianapanapa State Park.